Free for all

A celebration of 100 years of the Woolwich Free Ferry

by Julian Watson & Wendy Gregory

Greenwich Libraries
London Borough of Greenwich
1989

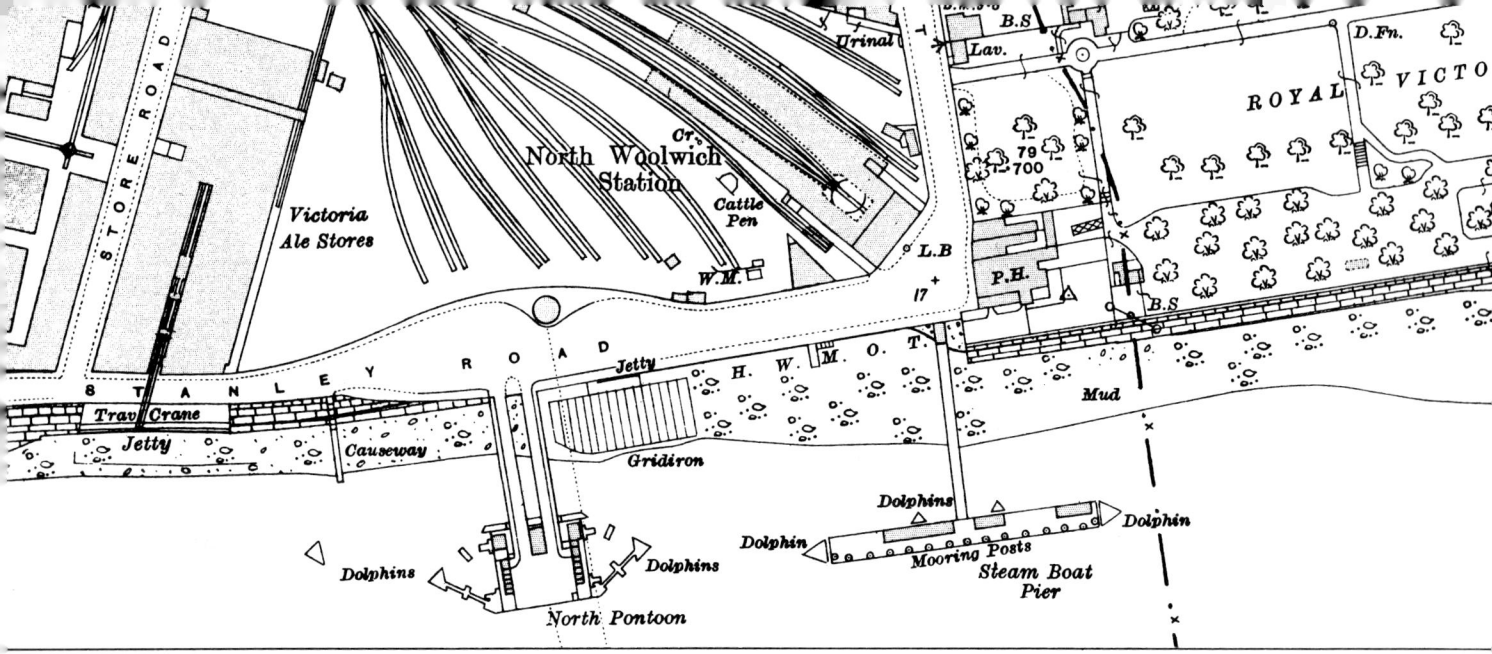

Acknowledgements

Publication of *Free for all* would not have been possible without the interest and support of Alex McIntosh, Assistant Director (Arts) at Greenwich Leisure, David Page, former ferry captain, and Peter Deeks and the staff of the Woolwich Free Ferry.

We are also grateful to many others for their help and advice, including: the staff of Greenwich Local History Library, Howard Bloch and the staff of Newham Libraries, Sydney Amas, Robert & Hazel Blayney, Peggy Bloomfield, John Brian, George Cooper, Lil Cooper, Winifred Cutler, Janet Desborough, Stella Drew, Joe Eaton, A E Elleston, Norman Emery, John Fisher, John Freeman, Eileen Giffin, George Gosling, Alec Green, Ruth Grummett, Sid Holmes, Steve Hunt, Maureen James, Frank Johnson, Tony Johnson, Patricia Leigh, Wendy McCarthy, Peter Middleton, Sylvia Montgomery, Bill Mulrenan, Kitty Murphy, Jenny O'Keefe, Harry Pearce, Peter Rand, Bill Shirett, Norman Smith, Tom Surry, George Taylor, Sylvia Taylor, Jack Tarrant, Jack Tyler, Harry White and Ivy Winchester.

Designed by Kit Gregory
Edited by Wendy Gregory
Typeset by Blackheath Photoset
Printed by E G Bond Ltd

ISBN 0 904399 08 7

© Copyright London Borough of Greenwich

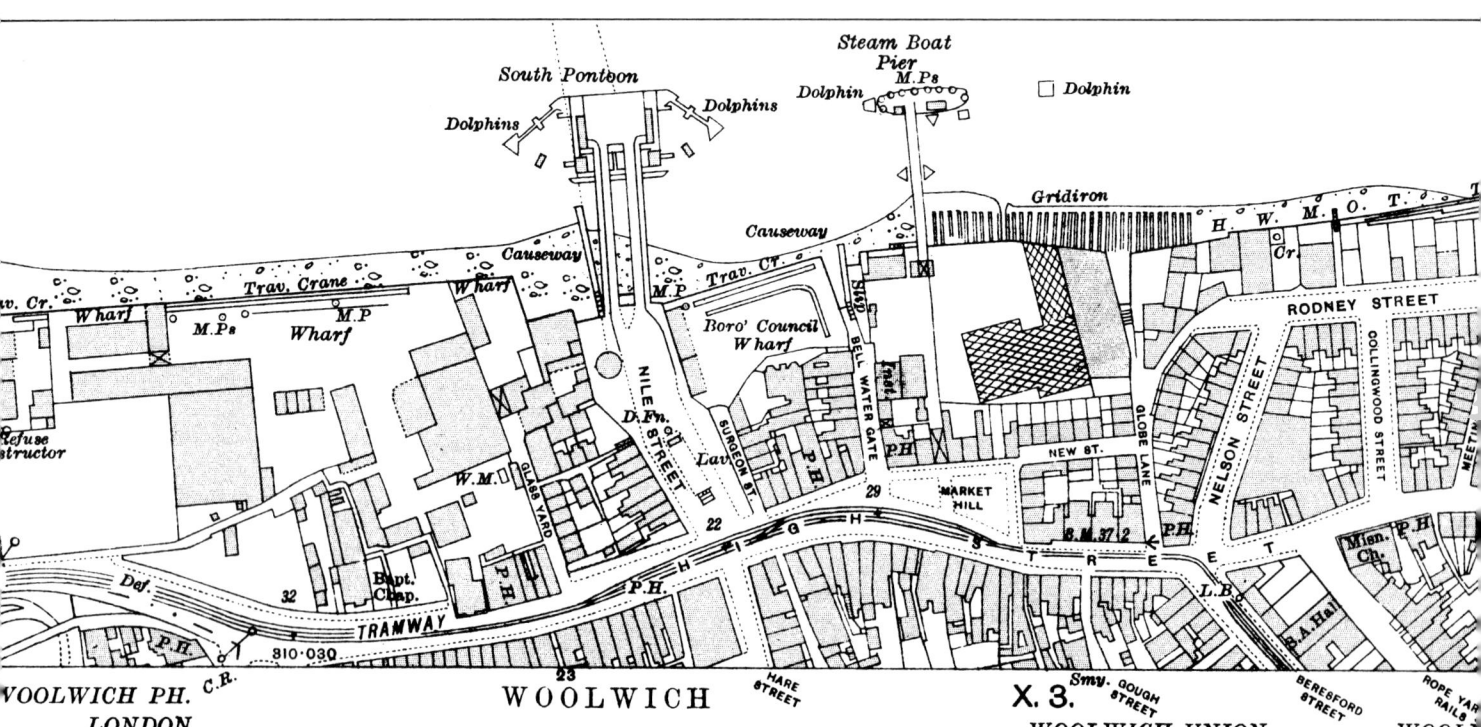

First ferries

Contents

2 Ordnance Survey map of 1916 showing north and south banks of the Thames.
3 First ferries: six centuries of river crossings at Woolwich before the advent of the Free Ferry.
5 Building up steam: demand grows for a free ferry service.
6 The *Gordon*: first in a proud line.
7 Free launch: the inaugural ceremony.
10 Paddle days: story of the steamers.
11 The *Hutton* and the *Duncan*.
12 The *Squires* and the *Gordon*.
13 The *Will Crooks* and the *John Benn*.
14 Captains and crews: life on board.
16 The paddle steamers: the romance of the steam boats.
18 Livestock afloat: it wasn't only people who used the ferries.
20 The vehicle deck: goods and traffic.
22 Out of steam and into diesel: the modern boats arrive on the river.
24 The diesel boats. The *James Newman* and the *John Burns*.
25 The *Ernest Bevin*.
26 Piers and approaches: a history of the terminals.
30 Free ferry fun: a good day out.

The name of Woolwich is well known throughout the country because of its Arsenal, building society, and now relocated football club. However, an equally famous feature of the town is its ferry service, unique in that it has provided free passage across the Thames for 100 years. Since 23 March 1889 when Lord Rosebery led the inaugural celebrations, the ferry has given outstanding service to Londoners and others, offering safety, reliability and, to many generations of local people, romantic memories of carefree days spent riding to and fro on the picturesque old paddle steamers.

Other ferry services at Woolwich predate the Free Ferry by hundreds of years; indeed, the existence of a crossing linking the two halves of the town may well be as old as the settlement itself. No other town on the lower reaches of the Thames straddles the river, it is a feature which has given Woolwich a unique strategic importance.

The crossing has provided a convenient link between the ancient highways from London to Dover and London to Colchester for many centuries. The fascinating discovery recently of a Roman fort and an Iron Age settlement on the riverside at Woolwich not only highlights the antiquity and historic importance of the area, but also suggests that a river crossing here may be considerably older than anyone had previously guessed.

For centuries, watermen ferried travellers across the river from Warren Lane, but few details survive. The earliest records indicate a surge of economic activity in Woolwich during the 14th century and provide rare evidence of early ferry business. The ferry was sold in 1308 by William de Wicton and his wife Roesia to William atte Hall; in 1320-1, Lambert de Trykenham sold it to John and Joan Latimer; and in 1340 Thomas Harwold bought the ferry from William and Mary Filliol for 100 marks (about £66) – a considerable increase on the £10 paid in 1308. Two North Woolwich deeds also refer to the ferry: one of 1346-7 mentions Carteris Lane, the street leading to "Wolwyche Verye", the other of 1348-9 refers to a croft on the road to "La Verie".

Not only was owning the ferry a sound investment in the early days, its existence must also have been important to the economy of the town as a whole and so had to be defended from any damaging competition. In 1330, Woolwich people petitioned the Crown for rival ferries at Greenwich and Erith to be suppressed. They strengthened their argument by emphasising that their ferry was "farmed of the King", in other words it was a royal ferry and part of the Manor of Eltham (the then equivalent of today's Sandringham). But the petition does not appear to have been successful, because a ferry continued to run at Greenwich for many centuries afterwards.

Until the Arsenal Ferry was set up in 1810 to transport artillery to Essex and the short-lived Woolwich Ferry Company started the following year, records of ferry services after the mid-14th century are few. The most notable reference being a petition by John Blount to King James I in 1622 asking him to grant a patent or lease for a long and short ferry at Woolwich.

The Woolwich Ferry Company was established by Act of Parliament in 1811 to carry passengers from Old Ballast Wharf on the Charlton/Woolwich boundary to the Plaistow Marshes. It was a hopeless venture, the company constructed expensive access roads on both sides of the river and provided two public houses: the Prince Regent on the north bank and the Marquis of Wellington on the south, for the use of passengers. However, the ferry was in such a remote spot people didn't bother to use it, and so the investment was never justified. The final blow came with the revelation that the ferry was illegally occupying land on the south bank belonging to the Bowater Estate. Deprived of a southern base, the company wound itself up in 1842.

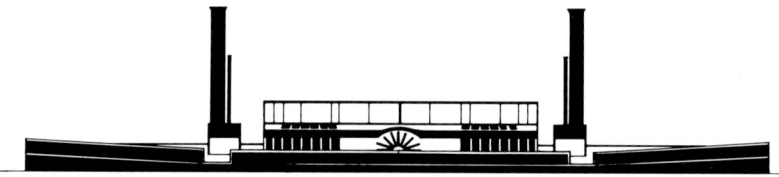

Building up steam

The decline of the Woolwich Ferry Company seems to have acted as a spur to the watermen operating the original service from Warren Lane to the "Barge House". In 1839, it was reported that "The lessees of the Woolwich Ferry have within the last few weeks stationed here a ferry boat of larger dimensions than any on the river, with a view to meeting the immense increase of traffic...".

The new-found fortune was short-lived however. Serious competition to the traditional ferry services arrived when the Great Eastern Railway Company started a regular steam ferry operation from their terminus at North Woolwich. The intention was to lure South Woolwich dwellers across the river to use the railway to London. Until 1849, when the North Kent Line came through Woolwich, there was no railway station in the southern half of the town. Thus, the "Penny Ferry", which operated from Roff's Wharf, offered a swift, cheap and regular service to local people until 1908. It was finally crushed by relentless competition from the Woolwich Free Ferry which had by this time been running for almost 20 years and which could carry horse traffic as well as people. The other ferry, or "horse raft", at Warren Lane which had held the monopoly on carrying horses and cattle for many years had been immediately put out of business with the advent of the Free Ferry.

The three steamboats of the Great Eastern Railway Company – *Kent, Essex* and *Middlesex* – had carried people quickly across the river, but vehicles and animals had to be transported on the old horse raft, so there was pressure on the local authority (the Woolwich Board of Health) to pay for a steam-driven vehicle ferry. A public meeting was held in Woolwich Town Hall in October 1880, and a year later 60 local traders lobbied the authority again.

The Board of Health duly carried out the necessary surveys and drew up estimates but found the scheme too

The Thames used to be much busier than it is today, but there were slack periods. The barges moored at "Starvation Buoys" were not working and indicate lean times for those whose living depended on transporting goods on the river.

expensive. Rather than reject it out of hand, they approached the Metropolitan Board of Works, the forerunner of the London County Council (LCC), proposing that the Metropolitan Board set up a steam ferry service at Woolwich. The local authority members astutely pointed out that as 11 bridges in London had recently been freed from tolls at a cost of £1.4 million to London's ratepayers, the new ferry should also be provided free. The idea was at first ridiculed, but the Board was eventually persuaded. An Act of Parliament, "The Metropolitan Board of Works (Various Powers) Act", in 1885 gave the Board the power to acquire land for the approaches and terminals, to operate the ferry free of all tolls and charges and to pay compensation to the private ferry operators and watermen who would be unable to compete with a free ferry.

This was the first in a series of free river crossings in the area: Blackwall Tunnel opened in 1897, Greenwich Foot Tunnel in 1902, and Woolwich Foot Tunnel in 1912.

All the planning and construction of the ferry service was carried out by the Metropolitan Board of Works but they were never to get credit or glory for their work as they were replaced by the LCC two days before the grand opening of the ferry in 1889. It was Lord Rosebery, Chairman of the LCC, who attended the inaugural ceremony and formally opened the Free Ferry on 23 March, not his predecessor on the Metropolitan Board who had managed the project.

On the opening day, only the *Gordon* was working, her sister ship the *Duncan* was not to be ready for service until 20 April when the *Gordon* was withdrawn for a short while to be fitted with electric lighting.

Seen here on the inaugural crossing, the *Gordon* served the Free Ferry until 1923 when she was replaced by the *Squires*. Built in 1888 by R & H Green, the *Gordon* was named after General Gordon of Khartoum (1833-1885), who was born in Woolwich and studied at the Academy.

Free launch

"A day the like of which few localities have upon their records, and one which for complete success has at no time or place been ever surpassed." So said William Thomas Vincent, Editor of the *Kentish Independent* about the celebrations on the day the Woolwich Free Ferry opened in 1889. This characteristic overstatement reveals the great pride that Vincent, Woolwich's greatest local historian, had in his adopted town. He was also reflecting the extreme excitement and joy that spread through the whole town during that weekend.

On the Friday night before the opening, the town was crowded with local people and with sightseers from further afield who had come to admire the lavishly decorated streets and colourful arrays of gas-light illuminations.

The inaugural celebrations began in the early afternoon of 23 March at the newly-built Freemasons' Hall in Mount Pleasant, now Masons Hill, where a magnificent triumphal arch, made of crossed poles and covered with evergreens and flowers, had been built by Messrs Lonergan, the builders. On the Woolwich side, the inscription made by a Burrage Grove schoolboy said "Welcome to Plumstead", on the other, "Success to the Ferry". Freemasons' Hall still retains much of its former splendour. Official parties from the Hall and from the Parish Offices in Maxey Road assembled by the Duke of Connaught Coffee Tavern in Woolwich New Road at 2.45pm to await the arrival of the London County Councillors who were travelling by train from London to Woolwich Arsenal station.

The procession was led through the town by mounted police. Volunteer soldiers from the 2nd Kent (Plumstead) Artillery, the 3rd Kent (Royal Arsenal) Rifles, the 3rd Kent (Royal Arsenal) Artillery and the bands of the Marine Society for Boys from the *Warspite* at Charlton joined groups from trade and friendly societies to parade through the streets.

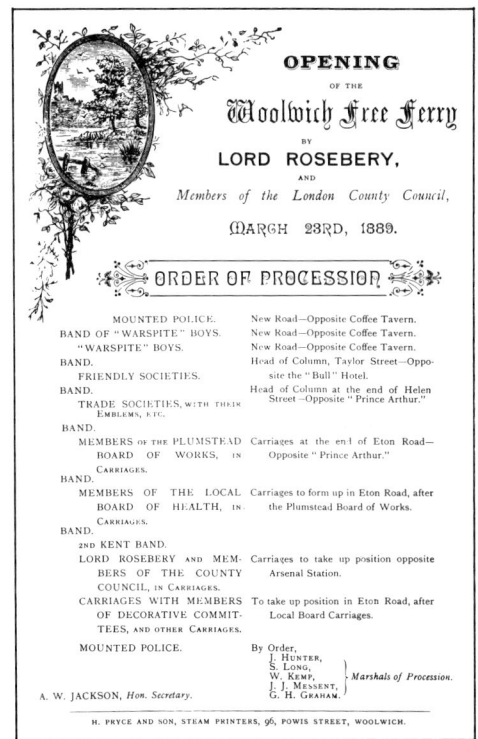

A card showing the Order of Procession on 23 March 1889.

Crowds thronged the streets of Woolwich as the procession made its way to the new ferry. The banners of the various societies made a colourful and lively spectacle.

Among the latter were the Ancient Order of Foresters, Oddfellows, Ancient Order of Britains, Carpenters and Joiners', Boilermakers', Bricklayers' and Masons' trade societies. The *Kentish Independent* also refers to "a few comical fellows" amid the colourful banners and uniforms. The mounted police brought up the rear.

Towards the back of the long and lively procession, the official party made their dignified way in about 40 vehicles through cheering crowds and down to the ferry terminal where Lord Rosebery's carriage drove straight on to the *Gordon's* vehicle deck. A mere three and a half minutes later, the official party were disembarking at North Woolwich, having been ably navigated across the river by Captain Young. The crowds were thinner on the north shore but they too gave a warm welcome to the first ever free travellers.

From the pier, the officials processed along High Street, Albert Road and Storey Street before returning to the ferry for the return journey. On the specially-built grandstand on the south shore Lord Rosebery made the long-awaited announcement to 600 invited guests: "In the name of the London County Council, I have the honour and pleasure of declaring this Free Ferry open to the public." Crowds then poured onto the *Gordon* to take advantage of the first free trips across the river.

The *Gordon,* which was the only boat in service that weekend (the *Duncan* was delivered later), worked unflaggingly in her first few days carrying the vast throngs of people who poured into Woolwich to see the new wonder. That weekend alone, the Great Eastern Railway Company carried 25,000 to its North Woolwich terminus – most of them intent on riding the ferry so that they could report in years to come that they had been there at the beginning.

The procession wound its way back up Hare Street, Powis Street and Thomas Street to Freemasons' Hall where a celebratory banquet was held for all the official party except Lord Rosebery who had had to return to London. The banquet, which was accompanied by many speeches and toasts, ended with a toast to the Metropolitan Board Officials who had been responsible for the planning and construction of the ferry but whose thunder had been stolen at the last minute by the LCC.

The next day, a Sunday, was a busy one for the *Gordon* and it was noted that "children, chiefly boys, were the warmest patrons". This state of affairs continued for many years as the paddle steamers proved an unfailing source of fascination for youngsters and their parents, not least because the boats provided an exciting but cheap day out.

Paddle days

The *Gordon, Duncan* and *Hutton* shared the same specifications despite the *Hutton* being built by a different company.

Cost	approx £15,000
Length	164 feet
Breadth	60 feet
Draught	4 feet
Tonnage	490 tons
Engines	2 pairs coal-fired diagonal surface-condensing engines
Speed	8 knots
Capacity	1000 passengers 15-20 vehicles

The essential character of the ferry service changed little between 1889 and 1963 when the paddle steamers were taken out of service. By 1930, the fleet consisted of four boats, the original three – *Gordon, Duncan* and *Hutton* – having given way to three more modern paddle steamers – *Squires,* the new *Gordon, Will Crooks* and *John Benn* – which were coke-fired in deference to London's increasingly polluted air.

The record of consistency and safety of the Woolwich Free Ferry has been remarkable. On only three occasions has the Free Ferry been closed for any length of time: for two weeks during the General Strike of 1926; for five weeks the same year when the *Squires* was hit and damaged by the US vessel *Coahoma City* while visiting the south ponton; and for three months in 1949 when the pontoons were taken into dry dock for repair. Even the great freeze of 1894-5 which paralysed much river traffic did not stop the ferry, nor did the bombing of two world wars.

It was during the bombing of the docks on 7 September 1940 that the ferries did heroic work rescuing families on the north shore and taking them across a river blazing with burning oil, to safety in Woolwich. Maybe it was confused reports of this rescue that gave rise to the commonly held but erroneous belief that the ferries had helped in the Dunkirk evacuation. Near misses from a bomb and a V1 rocket, coupled with navigation without lights in the blackout made war service on the ferries hazardous.

After World War II, increases in the number and size of road vehicles began to cause problems on the old paddle steamers, the positioning of modern articulated juggernauts proved tricky and, in some cases, impossible. Powis Street and Hare Street became congested with traffic waiting to board the ferry and pressure for action to relieve the situation grew locally.

Greater London Record Office

Like the *Gordon,* the *Duncan* was built in 1888 by R & H Green but didn't enter service until a month after her sister ship. She was named after Colonel Francis Duncan (1836-1888), the author of "The History of the Royal Artillery". Col Duncan, a soldier and an MP, was director of the St John's Ambulance Brigade from 1877-82. He died at Woolwich and is buried in Charlton.

Built in 1893 by William Simons & Co Ltd, the *Hutton* was named after Charles Hutton (1737-1823). A professor of Mathematics at Woolwich Academy from 1773-1807, Hutton calculated the density of the earth using measurements obtained in 1774 by the Astronomer Royal Nevil Maskeleyne.

The *Squires* and *Gordon* were both built by J Samuel White & Co Ltd in 1922 and had the same specification.

Cost	approx £35,000
Length	172 feet
Breadth	62 feet
Draught	4 feet 6 inches
Tonnage	625 tons
Engines	2 pairs coke-fired diagonal surface-condensing engines
Speed	8½ knots
Capacity	1000 passengers 15-20 vehicles

The *Squires* was named after William James Squires (1850-1931), a Woolwich man. Twice Mayor of Woolwich and for many years chairman of the Woolwich Equitable Building Society, Squires was a bookseller and stationer who owned two shops in the town.

The new *Gordon,* like her predecessor, was named after General Gordon of Khartoum.

Newham Libraries

The *Will Crooks* and the *John Benn* were also built by J Samuel White & Co Ltd, but did not join the *Squires* and the *Gordon* in service until 1930.

Cost	approx £37,000
Length	172 feet
Breadth	62 feet 0⅜ inches
Draught	4 feet 9 inches
Tonnage	625 tons
Engines	2 pairs coke-fired diagonal surface-condensing engines
Speed	8½ knots
Capacity	1000 passengers 15-20 vehicles

The *Will Crooks* was named after William Crooks (1852-1921), Woolwich's first Labour MP, who took his seat in the House of Commons in 1903. He also served on the LCC from 1892-1910, and was Mayor of Poplar in 1910.

The *John Benn* was named after Sir John Benn (1850-1922), ancestor of today's Tony Benn MP. A member of the LCC from its creation in 1889 and its chairman from 1904-05, he was also MP for Devonport for six years.

Captains and crews

If the engine room is the throbbing heart of the vessel, then the bridge is its brain. From here the Captain directs operations, controls the speed and direction of the ferry and keeps an eye on other river traffic.

The first ferries made scant provision for comfort. On *Gordon* and *Duncan* the Captain and Mate stood on the vehicle deck, exposed to the elements; *Hutton* was equipped with a rudimentary bridge, while *Squires*, the new *Gordon*, *Will Crooks* and *John Benn* were smarter, with lots of polished brass – but no heating.

Captains on the paddle steamers communicated with other boats by means of a steam whistle, and with the engine room by telegraphs – one for each paddle.

A captain and his crew around the turn of the century. As a public highway the ferries enjoyed the distinction of having their own policemen who included the ferry crossing as part of their regular beat until about 1950.

Today's propellers are controlled from any one of three consoles on the navigation bridge, but whistles are still used to communicate with other vessels.

Steering these huge ferries to and fro across half a mile of river may sound neither challenging nor interesting, but generations of Free Ferry Captains have defended their jobs as both. Vessels crossing the stream are obliged to give way to those travelling up and down river, the Thames at Woolwich is subject to strong tides and weather conditions must always be considered. With responsibility for so many lives and goods the Captain's work is both taxing and fulfilling.

Working on the ferries runs in families, often son follows father and grandfather onto the river, and many Captains started river life as humble deckhands.

The paddle steamers carried a crew of 14: Captain, Mate, Bosun, four deckhands, three engineers, two stokers, a greaser and a deck/cabin boy. Today's diesel vessels need fewer hands in the engine room and manage with a crew of seven: Captain, Mate, Engineer and four deckhands.

The day starts early, with the first shift's crew arriving by small boat an hour before the first crossing. They prepare the boat for the day ahead, and a lot of pride and effort goes into the cleaning and polishing. In the past, when there were more foot passengers, the crews knew many of their regular passengers personally and it was a matter of honour to keep the ferries spotless for them.

On the bridge of a paddle steamer:
Captain Sam Hudson, left, watches
ahead with Steve Barber the Mate,
while Bosun Jack Allan takes the wheel.

The paddle steamers

The beat of the paddles, the dominant "A" note of the telegraph, the singing and slapping of wet ropes and the metallic clang of the gangway being lowered; memories of the romantic paddle boats are as much to do with the sounds they made as with their imposing appearance.

At the end of the steam era, the seven boats had covered between them some 400,000 miles, crossing and re-crossing the Thames at Woolwich. They had carried 180 million passengers and 55 million vehicles and bicycles. Crews on the old boats got to know their regular passengers. The first crossings of the day saw dockers and factory workers come aboard; later, office staff and shop girls followed and then the shoppers themselves would flood across to Woolwich Market. Many found it cheaper and more convenient to live on one shore and work on the other.

But the ferries were not just a means of transport, it was also fun to watch the highly-polished engines turning over, to peer down the hatches into the crew's quarters or to watch the stokers, gleaming with sweat and stripped to the waist, feeding the vast red maw of the furnaces with coke. Bickering pigeons and gulls and passing river traffic provided entertainment on deck and the pungent scent of tobacco, hot oil and fresh paint captured many a young (and not so young) man's heart.

The ferries' independently-powered paddle wheels with their wooden floats made them suprisingly manoeuvrable, but floating and submerged debris could cause untold damage and the Master was constantly alert for such hazards. Objects which did entangle themselves had to be removed by reversing the direction of the paddle, with the help of a small boat, or by one of the engineers climbing right into the paddle box.

Livestock afloat

George Taylor

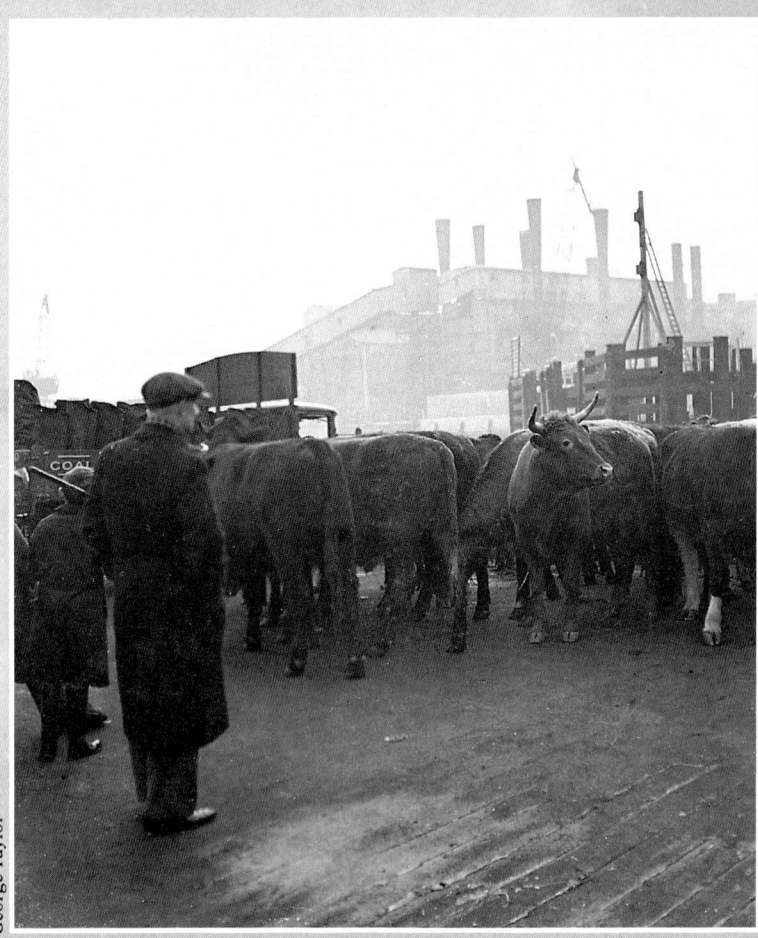

En route to the abattoir

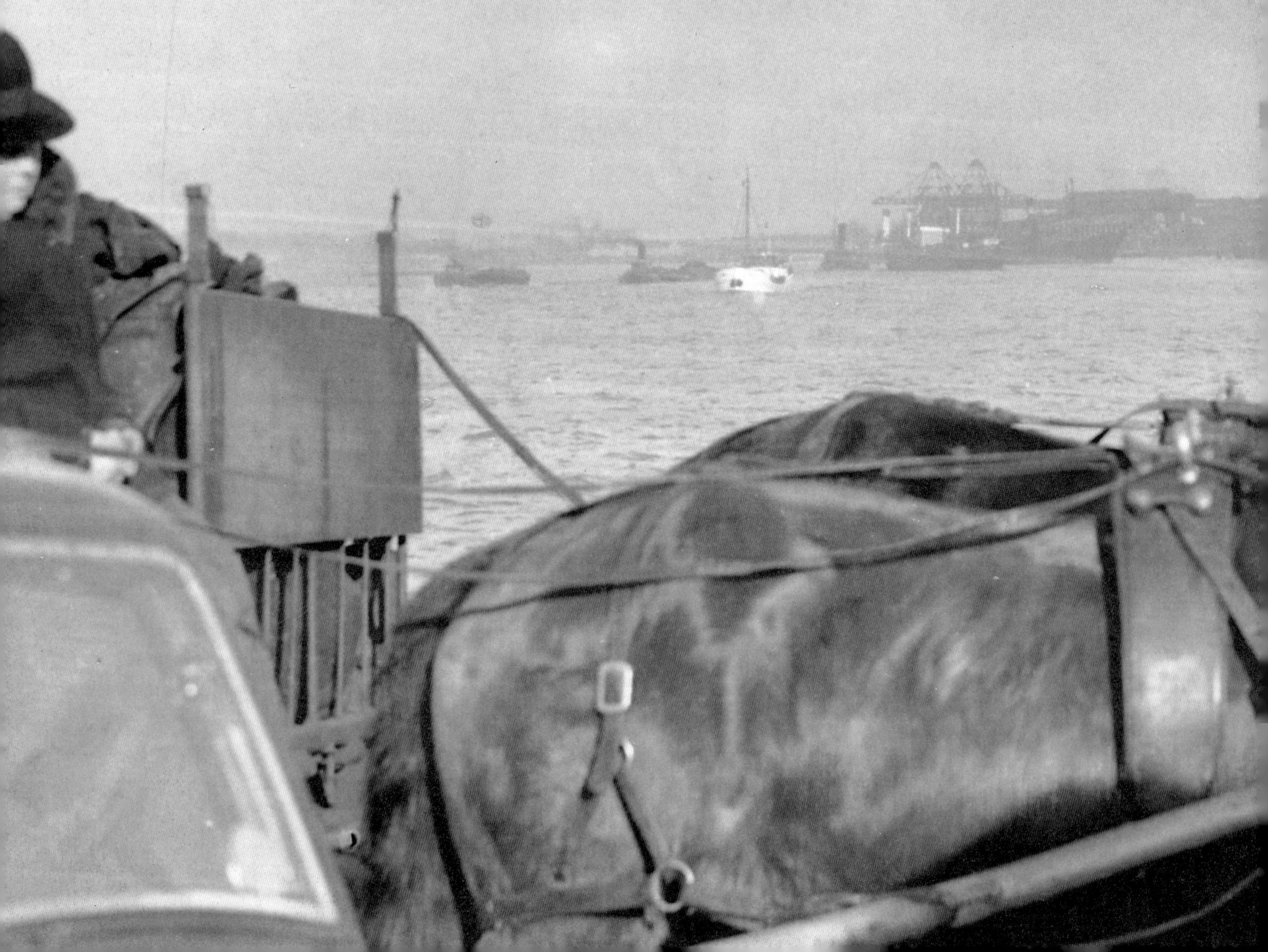

Unlike the Ark, the Woolwich Free Ferry has never restricted the numbers of its animal passengers. Herds of cows and flocks of sheep were regularly transported from North Woolwich Station to the south bank and thence to the RACS abattoir at Abbey Wood.

Horses were a common sight and, being well used to the crossing, usually positioned themselves correctly on deck without guidance. *The London* of 2 April 1896 reported however that "horses never look happy on the Ferry. Get a dozen of them on the upper deck, harnessed to their respective burdens – drays, vans, trolleys, carts and traps – and they always look like creatures losing courage." It was for these creatures that a "tracer" horse was kept to lead off the nervous.

In 1909, the young Handley Page carried his first aeroplane across the river in pieces in a horse-drawn cart, to be reassembled ready for its first test flight on the far side.

Frank Bryant, a skipper for many years, remembers his father telling him about rescuing a pig which had fallen overboard and for which the Co-op paid him half-a-crown (12½ pence).

During the '50s, a mongrel dog used the ferry to cross from north to south every day in order to fetch himself a bone from a butcher in Hare Street, and a ginger cat regularly came aboard, leaping the gap before the passenger ramp was completely down. Cats were always welcome as both ferries and pontoons had problems with rats.

In 1952, the circus came to the Free Ferry and, as the last elephant lumbered ashore, the cleaning-up process began. Always keen to bag up horse manure, gardeners among the crew vied with each other for a share of the day's jumbo-sized bonus.

John Topham Picture Library

The vehicle deck

Captain Sam Hudson surveys the vehicle deck from the bridge of the *Squires*. It is evident that as vehicles got taller visibility from the bridge would get more difficult.

For drivers, the Woolwich Ferry provides a pleasant respite from the rat race of the North and South Circular Roads which are joined at their eastern extremities by the ferry.

The paddle steamers carried fewer vehicles than the modern boats but even so clocked up 55 million cars and lorries before being replaced by the diesel boats.

It has always been the important task of the deckhands to direct traffic on the vehicle deck –

carefully judging and balancing weights to ensure even loading. A lop-sided craft would leave one paddle splashing ineffectively half out of the murky water.

All kinds of goods used to be transported but when vehicles carrying petrol or explosives required passage they travelled in stately solitude, with the ferry flying the "petrol flag" and no other vehicles or passengers being allowed on the same crossing. Today, dangerous loads must use the Dartford Tunnel.

The new boats have bridges high enough to see over even the largest trucks and the vehicle decks are capable of taking up to 200 tons of traffic.

The vehicle deck of the *John Burns* in 1963. The diesel boats are equipped with bridges which give maximum all-round visibility.

Out of steam and into diesel

Three new ships took over from the old paddle steamers in 1963. Built by The Caledon Shipbuilding & Engineering Co Ltd in Dundee, their remarkable design and revolutionary propulsion system gave great flexibility of movement, fast loading and indifference to the vagaries of wind and water. Thus they were far superior to the paddle steamers which had required great skill and understanding of "drift" to manoeuvre effectively. It did not take the seasoned captains long to master handling the new boats. They quickly taught themselves by practising on the river between Woolwich and Erith.

The *John Burns, Ernest Bevin* and *James Newman* came down from Scotland under their own power and started working from the old ferry terminals in 1963. They were designed as end-loaders, but until the new terminal and approach roads were completed in 1966, they functioned as side-loaders like their predecessors. The new ferries really came into their own, however, on 20 September 1966 when Rex Whitton, US Federal Highway Administrator (in London to attend the International Road Federation Conference) opened the new terminals on which the Greater London Council (GLC) had spent £2 million in order to bring them right up to date.

Traffic could now avoid the centre of Woolwich, travelling instead along a dual-carriageway which followed the line of Brewer Street and St John's Passage. The benefits of the new ferries were enormous, the efficiency and speed of loading unparalleled, but everyone agreed that the romance of the old steamers had gone.

The four universally-loved boats vanished almost without trace. They were sold to Messrs Jacques Bakker & Zonen in Zalzate, Belgium, for scrap. The sole surviving fragment being a bell rescued from the *John Benn* by the publishers Benn Brothers, a firm founded by Sir John William Benn after whom the boat was named. The bell was mounted on a stand designed by Lucian Ercolani, the eminent furniture designer, and is now displayed in Benn Brothers' offices. Thus an era of travel came to a swift end and even the brief emergence of a local pop group in 1971 named "Free Ferry" failed to conjure up the old atmosphere.

The ferry, under the direction of Greenwich Council since the GLC was disbanded in 1986, is now entering a period of uncertainty as it faces competition from the East London River Crossing – a bridge which will divert most of the cross-river traffic away from Woolwich. However, it is hoped it will be retained as a continuing amenity for Woolwich people and for the new communities which are springing up all over Dockland.

The diesel boats

The *James Newman* is named after James Newman (1879-1955), a distinguished citizen of Woolwich. A school teacher, he was Mayor of Woolwich 1923-25 and 1951-52. He was a member of Woolwich Council for many years, starting in 1906, and was co-founder and vice-President of the Woolwich Council of Social Services.

The most important innovation on the new diesel-engined boats was their Voith-Schneider Cycloidal Propellers, the first to appear on the river. These strange devices, looking more like five-legged coffee tables than conventional screw propellers have the great advantage of enabling the ferries to approach the terminals head on, whatever the tide. With a propeller at each end, the modern boats can travel in either direction, spin on the spot like a carousel or move sideways simply by altering the angle of the blades.

The diesel-powered ferries have already served 26 years and were built to run well into the next millennium. By January '89, the three boats – *John Burns*, *Ernest Bevin* and *James Newman* – had ferried 26 million cars and lorries on over a million crossings.

Newham Libraries

The *Ernest Bevin* is named after Ernest Bevin (1881-1951), pioneer of modern trade unionism. A minister in two governments and Labour MP for Woolwich during the last year of his life, Bevin was known affectionately as "the dockers' KC".

The *John Burns* is named after John Elliot Burns (1858-1943), who led the great dock strike of 1889 and went on to become, in 1905, the first artisan to reach Cabinet rank. An enthusiast of London's river, he coined the phrase "liquid history" to describe the Thames. The *John Burns* is the current flagship of the fleet.

The *John Burns*, *James Newman* and *Ernest Bevin* were all built in 1963 at The Caledon Shipbuilding and Engineering Co Ltd shipyards in Dundee, and they entered service the same year. The three diesel boats have maintained a reliable and efficient service ever since the end of the steam era.

Cost	approx £268,000
Length	185 feet 7 inches
Breadth	61 feet
Draught	6 feet
Tonnage	738½ tons
Engines	2 pressure-charged Mirrlees Blackstone 500 hp diesel engines drive 2 Voith-Schneider cycloidal propellers, one at each end of the boat
Capacity	500 passengers 200 tons of vehicles

Hog Lane, along with several other areas near the south approaches to the ferry, was demolished to provide better access for vehicles.

The south bank in the early '50s. The entrance to the Foot Tunnel can be seen in the right foreground. Many of the other buildings were later cleared to accommodate the modern terminals which were opened in 1966.

Piers and approaches

Building the ferry approaches in the 1880s had little effect on the emerging community of North Woolwich, but changes south of the river were more profound and provided an opportunity to demolish some of the worst slum housing in the notorious "Dusthole", an area of immense poverty.

The south terminal was at the end of one of Woolwich's most ancient streets. Hog Lane, full of neglected dwellings and low lodging houses was knocked together with Surgeon Street to form a wide access road, with plenty of space for passengers and vehicles waiting for the ferry.

From 1912, pedestrians wishing to cross the river had a choice: either they could wait for the ferry and enjoy a breezy ride across the busy river, or they could take a long walk through the newly-opened Foot Tunnel.

The floating pontoons which formed the original terminals were each supported on fifty air chambers, so passengers had the opportunity to gain their sea legs before boarding as the platforms responded to wind and waves.

The old landing stages measured 100 by 83 feet (30× 25m) and consisted of two platforms; the lower with four waiting rooms for pedestrians, the upper level for carts, wagons and carriages. J Mowlem & Co were responsible for preparing the landing places, Thames Iron Works constructed the bridges and pontoons, and Messrs Easton and Anderson provided the hydraulic machinery which operated the hinged "brows" that linked boat and pontoon.

For the thousands of travellers regularly using the ferries, there were plenty of shops, pubs and other distractions close to the ferry terminals and a variety of other means of transport were available to speed them on their way.

When the new terminals were built in the mid '60s, little disturbance was necessary in North Woolwich, but considerable disruption and demolition was again necessary on the south bank in order to build the pier, offices, workshops and

Traffic driving off the ferry and on to the north pier soon after the Second World War.

The *Duncan* calls at the south pontoon. The photograph is dated 27 July 1896.

Inspecting a damaged paddle float while a paddle steamer was on the grid. The wooden floats were particularly susceptible to damage by floating debris. One ferry is always "on the grid" for regular maintenance or repairs. The grid is a wooden platform on to which a boat can be floated on a flood tide and left high and dry as the waters recede. The grid used to be on the north bank, but moved to the south side when the new terminals were built.

waiting area. The attractive 18th-century Enon Baptist Chapel in the High Street was pulled down and "Forty Corners", an ancient right of way which twisted and turned behind the chapel, disappeared without trace – much to the chagrin of local children.

The new landing stages, designed for the County Council by Husband & Co and built by Marples, Ridgway and Partners, are fixed piers supported on piles. They are linked to the ferries by hinged loading ramps operated from huge hoist towers. These "link spans" have to deal with large fluctuations in the level of the river: on the north side the water is about 16 feet deep at low water spring tide and only about five feet (1.5m) on the south side. But the spring tidal variation is between 21 and 23 feet (6.3 - 6.9m), and can be as much as a formidable 30 feet (9m). Thus passengers may travel steeply up or down onto the ferries.

Unlike the old ferries, the modern vessels end-load – the traffic rolling on one end and off at the other. The diesel boats are held in place at the terminals by engine power alone and do not need mooring with ropes as did the paddle steamers. Both these facilities contribute greatly to the speed of the turn round.

The new terminals have enabled the ferry service to cope with vastly increased traffic levels and facilitate a very swift crossing, and many local people were impressed by the new river views which were opened up with the demolition of the old buildings. However, the romance of the crossing died with the passing of the paddle steamers and the homely hubbub of the old Ferry Approach (now compeletly buried under the Waterfront Leisure Centre), with its small shops and bustle of trams and trolley buses, could never be recaptured by the modern efficient approches dominated by what D J D Wood so aptly described as "reinforced concrete monoliths."

Free ferry fun

"If there is any place in the boat where they ought not to be...the boys of a certainty will discover it," said *The London* in 1896. Since the ferry started, children have delighted in chasing around the decks, taunting the constables, evading the crews. Watching the stokers, chatting to the engineers, feeding the pigeons, the ferries have given 100 years of fun and fascination.

But it's not always fun – children have been known to fall overboard and for the youngsters who worked as deckhands in the early days, life was an endless round of cleaning and errand running.

Many passengers took the boats for granted while enjoying their facilities. Families used to take a picnic aboard for a free day out and half an hour on deck was once considered a wonderful whooping cough cure. There was always something to watch and on chilly days passengers would compete for space on the warm boiler casings.

It was always exciting when the river was busy. The ferries would get as close as possible to passing large ships in order to nip under the stern before another vessel blocked the way.

Greater London Record Office

John Topham Picture Library

John Topham Picture Library

31

I remember...

...the sights...the sounds...the smells...the steam...
the paddles...the piers...the pontoons...the pigeons...
the fun...